THE BOOK
21 Day
HABIT

Tyndale House Publishers, Inc.
WHEATON, ILLINOIS

Visit Tyndale's exciting Web site at www.tyndale.com

Notes and introduction written by Jerry and Edie Wasserberg for the
Christian Broadcasting Network.

Scripture quotations are taken from the *Holy Bible,* New Living Translation, copyright © 1996. Used by permission of Tyndale House Publishers,
Inc., Wheaton, Illinois 60189. All rights reserved.

New Living and the New Living Translation logo are registered trademarks
of Tyndale House Publishers, Inc.

The Book and *The Book* logo are registered trademarks of The Christian
Broadcasting Network, Inc.

ISBN 0-8423-3581-1

Printed in the United States of America

05   04   03   02   01   00   99
10   9   8   7   6   5   4   3   2   1

CONTENTS

INTRODUCTION

You are not alone!

Did you know that

- Eighty-two percent of Americans feel the need in their lives to experience spiritual growth.
- Six in ten Americans say religion is very important in their lives (the highest percentage in recent decades).
- Half of all Americans fear being unforgiven by God or cut off from God's love when they die.

Gallup and Barna poll, 1998

Millions of people across America are searching for greater meaning in their lives. Busy schedules, family and work demands, concerns for the future, and disappointments from the past—all of these contribute to this longing for inner peace.

The Book: 21 Day Habit can help you find that peace and guidance. You have taken the first step on your journey to a richer life and brighter tomorrow. You are about to take control of your time in a life-changing way. Something good is entering your life, and as you apply its principles, you will never be the same.

Why The Book: 21 Day Habit?

Have you ever considered the importance of habit in your life? Habits allow us to move through our day without having to stop and make a conscious decision over each action. For instance, many of us had a cup of coffee this morning, brushed our teeth, and combed our hair—all without having to decide whether or not we would or should. We did it simply because it is our habit to do so. Habits can help us or hurt us, as this poem illustrates:

THE POWER OF HABIT

I am your constant companion.
I am your greatest helper or your heaviest
    burden.
I will push you onward or drag you down to
    failure.
I am completely at your command.
Half the things you do you might as well turn
    over to me,
And I will be able to do them quickly and cor-
    rectly.
I am easily managed; you must merely be firm
    with me.

Show me exactly how you want something
   done,
And after a few lessons I will do it automati-
   cally.
I am the servant of all great individuals
And, alas, of all failures as well.
Those who are great I have made great.
Those who are failures I have made failures.
I am not a machine, though I work with all the
   precision of a machine
Plus the intelligence of a human being.
You may run me for profit or run me for ruin;
It makes no difference to me.
Take me, train me, be firm with me,
And I will put the world at your feet.
Be easy with me, and I will destroy you.
Who am I?
I am habit!

Author Unknown

What Is The Book: 21 Day Habit?

The Book: 21 Day Habit brings together some
of the most effective motivators in behavioral
sciences today and joins them to the most powerful words in the world, the Word of God.

God's Word makes some extraordinary claims
about itself. God says his Word is alive and full
of power. It can cut through to your innermost
thoughts and desires and expose your deepest

longings and truest motives. God's Word is full of promises—promises that don't lie but that stand ready to help you as you call on them in your daily life. In this booklet you will be reading from *The Book,* a new, easy-to-read and easy-to-understand translation of the Bible.

As far as effective motivators, behaviorists tell us that when we are involved in a purposeful, goal-oriented behavior, we have an increased sense of well-being and worth. *The Book: 21 Day Habit* is such a behavior. Each day that you read, you will be achieving your goal. In addition, your mind will be receiving powerful, positive insights. These positive words will affect your thinking and outlook. Say them to yourself again and again, and see the changes that occur in your life, your family, and your attitude.

Behavioral science has determined that repeating a behavior for 21 days develops a habit. In just 21 days, you will have taken control of your time and built into your life a habit that will bring you peace, joy, and guidance.

It's up to you. One day at a time. Commit now to take charge. Millions of people all over America are making the same decision to add goodness and strength to their lives. God wants to give you something special. He has words for your heart alone. Come and experience his incredible love and presence. Join in *The Book: 21 Day Habit.* Life will never be the same again.

The 21 Days
Through national focus-group testing, men and women were asked what issues were of concern in their lives today. The same concerns were repeated consistently in all the groups. Those concerns are addressed in *The Book: 21 Day Habit.* Each day covers a new concern and gives related counsel and guidance from God's Word.

How to Begin
Each day's reading is organized into four parts:

- First, a brief introduction to the day's topic.
- Second, selected portions from *The Book* that relate to the issue of the day.
- Third, God's Promise—a promise from God himself, relating the topic to life.
- Last, an Action Point, giving a suggested action or way we can incorporate what we have learned into our daily life.

Set aside a few minutes each day, preferably at the same time every day. Make an appointment with yourself. Write it on your calendar. Be firm with family and friends so that you will not be interrupted. Practice the action point! There is great learning that occurs when we put a new truth into practice. If you are able, review your reading several times each day. You are strength-training your soul, and repetition will build eternal muscle.

Day **1**

THE WORD OF GOD

All of us long to hear a good word—a word of comfort, a word of encouragement, a word of love. We bloom in the environment of positive words, while harsh words cause us to shrivel. Sometimes we say we are tired of words, when in fact we are tired of empty words, of broken words. We long for a life-giving word that will not fail.

FROM **THE BOOK**

God is not a man, that he should lie. He is not a human, that he should change his mind. Has he ever spoken and failed to act? Has he ever promised and not carried it through? *Numbers 23:19,* page 172

The word of God is full of living power. It is sharper than the sharpest knife, cutting deep into our innermost thoughts and desires. It exposes us for what we really are. *Hebrews 4:12,* page 1210

The grass withers, and the flowers fade beneath the breath of the LORD. And so it is with people. The grass withers, and the flowers fade, but the word of our God stands forever. *Isaiah 40:7-8,* page 713

GOD'S PROMISE

Keep on asking, and you will be given what you ask for. Keep on looking, and you will find. Keep on knocking, and the door will be opened. For everyone who asks, receives. Everyone who seeks, finds. And the door is opened to everyone who knocks. *Matthew 7:7-8,* page 937

ACTION POINT

Maybe you're not sure about God and the Bible, but you've already taken the first step. So for the next twenty days, tell God you're here and that you're ready for whatever he shows you in *The Book*.

Day 2
LOVE

So many singers sing about it. So many writers write about it. Poets long for it, and heroes die for it. What is this thing that the world needs now? Love! As human beings, we all need to love and be loved. God made us to experience love, and God, the source of love, can fill our need for love as no other person or idea can.

FROM **THE BOOK**

Dear friends, let us continue to love one another, for love comes from God. Anyone who loves is born of God and knows God. But anyone who does not love does not know God—for God is love.

God showed how much he loved us by sending his only Son into the world so that we might have eternal life through him. This is real love. It is not that we loved God, but that he loved us and sent his Son as a sacrifice to take away our sins.

Dear friends, since God loved us that much, we surely ought to love each other. *1 John 4:7-11,* page 1239

If I had the gift of prophecy, and if I knew all the mysteries of the future and knew everything about everything, but didn't love others, what good would I be? And if I had the gift of faith so that I could speak to a mountain and make it move, without love I would be no good to anybody. If I gave everything I have to the poor and even sacrificed my body, I could boast about it; but if I didn't love others, I would be of no value whatsoever.

Love is patient and kind. Love is not jealous or boastful or proud or rude. Love does not demand its own way. Love is not irritable, and it keeps no record of when it has been wronged. It is never glad about injustice but rejoices whenever the truth wins out. Love never gives up, never loses faith, is always hopeful, and endures through every circumstance. *1 Corinthians 13:2-7,* page 1148

GOD'S PROMISE

I have loved you, my people, with an ever-lasting love. With unfailing love I have drawn you to myself. *Jeremiah 31:3,* page 768

ACTION POINT

Tell someone today that you love him or her, not with your words but with your actions. Tear up that list of wrongs you've been keeping, and believe and hope the best about those you love. Your feelings will soon follow your actions.

Day 3

FORGIVENESS

Sometimes the most difficult people to forgive are ourselves. "If only" hounds us, robbing us of peace and piling on the guilt. We carry around 1,001 hurts and bear so many grudges, filling us with bitterness. Oh, to be cleansed and freed—to forgive and be forgiven!

FROM **THE BOOK**

"Come now, let us argue this out," says the LORD. "No matter how deep the stain of your sins, I can remove it. I can make you as clean as freshly fallen snow. Even if you are stained as red as crimson, I can make you as white as wool." *Isaiah 1:18,* page 681

He has removed our rebellious acts as far away from us as the east is from the west. *Psalm 103:12,* page 617

You must make allowance for each other's faults and forgive the person who offends you. Remember, the Lord forgave you, so you must forgive others. *Colossians 3:13, page 1186*

Get rid of all bitterness, rage, anger, harsh words, and slander, as well as all types of malicious behavior. Instead, be kind to each other, tenderhearted, forgiving one another, just as God through Christ has forgiven you. *Ephesians 4:31-32, page 1176*

GOD'S PROMISE
If we confess our sins to him, he is faithful and just to forgive us and to cleanse us from every wrong. *1 John 1:9, page 1236*

ACTION POINT
English poet Alexander Pope wrote, "To err is human, to forgive divine." Ask God today to help you get free from your load of hurts and anger. Start by accepting God's forgiveness, and then try giving it away to someone today.

TRIALS AND TEMPTATIONS

"You just have to play the hand you're dealt." "Keep a stiff upper lip." It's the advice we get and give when times are tough. Others would have us pretend that "it's not as bad as all that." But sometimes it is! So how can we remain hopeful when troubles surround us? When we recognize that God is in control!

FROM **THE BOOK**

Evil does not spring from the soil, and trouble does not sprout from the earth. People are born for trouble as predictably as sparks fly upward from a fire. *Job 5:6-7, page 545*

We know that God causes everything to work together for the good of those who love God and are called according to his purpose for them. *Romans 8:28, page 1125*

Our present troubles are quite small and won't last very long. Yet they produce for us an immeasurably great glory that will last forever! So we don't look at the troubles we can see right now; rather, we look forward to what we have not yet seen. For the troubles we see will soon be over, but the joys to come will last forever. *2 Corinthians 4:17-18,* page 1157

GOD'S PROMISE

Remember that the temptations that come into your life are no different from what others experience. And God is faithful. He will keep the temptation from becoming so strong that you can't stand up against it. When you are tempted, he will show you a way out so that you will not give in to it. *1 Corinthians 10:13,* page 1145

ACTION POINT

Today, when a trial or temptation comes your way, *stop!* Ask God to show you a way through the trial or away from the temptation. Then follow his direction, and experience the victory you have in him.

JESUS: WHO HE IS

He remains the most intriguing, controversial figure in all of history. A simple carpenter from a backwater town in a tiny country—yet a man who split time in two, uniting God and man in one body. Son of God, Son of Man, Jesus.

FROM **THE BOOK**

In the beginning the Word already existed. He was with God, and he was God. He was in the beginning with God. . . . So the Word became human and lived here on earth among us. He was full of unfailing love and faithfulness. And we have seen his glory, the glory of the only Son of the Father. *John 1:1-2, 14,* page 1044

She will have a son, and you are to name him Jesus, for he will save his people from their sins." *Matthew 1:21,* page 930

Now in these final days, he has spoken to us through his Son. God promised everything to the Son as an inheritance, and through the Son he made the universe and everything in it. The Son reflects God's own glory, and everything about him represents God exactly. He sustains the universe by the mightly power of his command. After he died to cleanse us from the stain of sin, he sat down in the place of honor at the right hand of the majestic God of heaven. *Hebrews 1:2-3, page 1207*

GOD'S PROMISE

I am the way, the truth, and the life. No one can come to the Father except through me. *John 14:6, page 1065*

ACTION POINT

A jailer asked the apostle Paul what he must do to be saved. Paul replied, "Believe on the Lord Jesus, and you will be saved" (see Acts 16:22-34). The answer is the same today as it was then. What must you do about Jesus? Believe. Believe, and you, too, will be saved.

JESUS: WHAT HE DID

Why did Jesus come? Was it merely to be an example—an impossibly perfect one at that? What was the Good News he preached? Why was this good man horribly executed like a common criminal? Did he come to fulfill a divine plan? Did he die to show the Father's love and live again three days later to give eternal life to anyone who would accept his leadership?

FROM **THE BOOK**

The Spirit of the Lord is upon me, for he has appointed me to preach Good News to the poor. He has sent me to proclaim that captives will be released, that the blind will see, that the downtrodden will be freed from their oppressors, and that the time of the Lord's favor has come. *Luke 4:18,* page 1006

Even I, the Son of Man, came here not to be served but to serve others, and to give my life as a ransom for many. *Mark 10:45,* page 987

"When we get to Jerusalem," he told them, "the Son of Man will be betrayed to the leading priests and the teachers of religious law. They will sentence him to die and hand him over to the Romans. They will mock him, spit on him, beat him with their whips, and kill him, but after three days he will rise again." *Mark 10:33-34, page 987*

From prison and trial they led him away to his death. But who among the people realized that he was dying for their sins—that he was suffering their punishment? *Isaiah 53:8, page 725*

GOD'S PROMISE

If you confess with your mouth that Jesus is Lord and believe in your heart that God raised him from the dead, you will be saved. *Romans 10:9, page 1127*

ACTION POINT

If you're convinced that Jesus came to die to pay for your sins, go ahead and thank him. And then tell a friend that you've become a child of God.

Day **7**

DISCOURAGEMENT/ DEPRESSION

Most of us have felt discouragement at some point in our life. When discouragement continues, depression results, and we become mired in dejection. But sometimes just the presence of a friend who is willing to listen can lift us up. God is such a friend, and he is always willing to listen when we call out to him.

FROM **THE BOOK**

The LORD is a shelter for the oppressed, a refuge in times of trouble. Those who know your name trust in you, for you, O LORD, have never abandoned anyone who searches for you. *Psalm 9:9-10, page 572*

"I know the plans I have for you," says the LORD. "They are plans for good and not for disaster, to give you a future and a hope. In those days when you pray, I will listen. If you look for me in earnest, you will find me when you seek me. I will be found by you," says the LORD. *Jeremiah 29:11-14,* page 766

We have a great High Priest who has gone to heaven, Jesus the Son of God. Let us cling to him and never stop trusting him. This High Priest of ours understands our weaknesses, for he faced all of the same temptations we do, yet he did not sin. So let us come boldly to the throne of our gracious God. There we will receive his mercy, and we will find grace to help us when we need it. *Hebrews 4:14-16,* page 1210

GOD'S PROMISE

Jesus said, "Come to me, all of you who are weary and carry heavy burdens, and I will give you rest. Take my yoke upon you. Let me teach you, because I am humble and gentle, and you will find rest for your souls. For my yoke fits perfectly, and the burden I give you is light." *Matthew 11:28-30,* page 943

ACTION POINT

What a friend we have in Jesus! Take time today to tell him what is discouraging you. He will exchange your heavy burden for true rest and peace for your soul.

Day **8**

GOD THE FATHER

Whether you had a great dad or a not-so-great dad, you can at least picture how a loving father acts toward his children. With love, compassion, and wisdom, he guides and corrects them, enabling them to live rich and full lives.

FROM **THE BOOK**

The LORD is like a father to his children, tender and compassionate to those who fear him. *Psalm 103:13,* page 617

Father to the fatherless, defender of widows—this is God, whose dwelling is holy. *Psalm 68:5,* page 599

Surely you are still our Father! Even if Abraham and Jacob would disown us, LORD, you would still be our Father. You are our Redeemer from ages past. *Isaiah 63:16,* page 732

My child, don't ignore it when the LORD disciplines you, and don't be discouraged when he corrects you. For the LORD corrects those he loves, just as a father corrects a child in whom he delights. *Proverbs 3:11-12,* page 641

GOD'S PROMISE

Don't worry about having enough food or drink or clothing. Why be like the pagans who are so deeply concerned about these things? Your heavenly Father already knows all your needs, and he will give you all you need from day to day if you live for him and make the Kingdom of God your primary concern. *Matthew 6:31-33,* page 937

ACTION POINT

List the ten best characteristics you can think of in a great father. Now read the list again, and know that God the Father is all of that and more. He is your perfect Father, and he is ready, willing, and able to love you with perfect love.

THANKSGIVING

What difference do you think it made when the Pilgrims invited the Native Americans to that first Thanksgiving dinner? What happened after they thanked God, who supplied the fish, the deer, and the corn—and even the Native Americans who helped them survive? Did life become significantly easier or the winters less cruel? No. But the attitude of gratitude that was cultivated kept those Pilgrims' eyes fixed upon the many blessings they enjoyed and upon the one who provided them.

FROM **THE BOOK**

Give thanks to the LORD, for he is good!
Psalm 136:1, page 633

Don't worry about anything; instead, pray about everything. Tell God what you need, and thank him for all he has done. If you do this, you will experience God's peace, which is far more wonderful than the human mind can understand. His peace will guard your hearts and minds as you live in Christ Jesus. *Philippians 4:6-7,* page 1182

No matter what happens, always be thankful, for this is God's will for you who belong to Christ Jesus. *1 Thessalonians 5:18,* page 1191

GOD'S PROMISE

Enter his gates with thanksgiving; go into his courts with praise. Give thanks to him and bless his name. For the LORD is good. His unfailing love continues forever, and his faithfulness continues to each generation. *Psalm 100:4-5,* page 616

ACTION POINT

Make a list of things that you can say thank you to God about, and give him a "thanksgiving feast." Then make a list of things you're worried about. As you ask God to provide for these things as well, thank him again.

PEACE WITH GOD

July 4, 1776: Thirteen American colonies declared their independence from Great Britain, setting off the war necessary to gain that freedom. In the same way, when we declare our independence from God, we set ourselves at war with him. Who can negotiate the peace?

FROM **THE BOOK**

God is not a mortal like me, so I cannot argue with him or take him to trial. If only there were a mediator who could bring us together, but there is none. *Job 9:32-33,* page 548

Listen! The LORD is not too weak to save you, and he is not becoming deaf. He can hear you when you call. But there is a problem—your sins have cut you off from God. Because of your sin, he has turned away and will not listen anymore. *Isaiah 59:1-2,* page 729

He was wounded and crushed for our sins. He was beaten that we might have peace. He was whipped, and we were healed! All of us have strayed away like sheep. We have left God's paths to follow our own. Yet the LORD laid on him the guilt and sins of us all. *Isaiah 53:5-6, page 725*

GOD'S PROMISE

Since we have been made right in God's sight by faith, we have peace with God because of what Jesus Christ our Lord has done for us. *Romans 5:1, page 1121*

ACTION POINT

Jesus can end your war and bring you peace with God. Ask him to do it. Thank him for taking your penalty for sin and independence from God. Ask God to give you his peace today.

HEAVEN/ETERNAL LIFE

Imagine the most beautiful place you have ever seen. Is it the red mountains of Sedona? the azure blue of the Pacific as it pounds against rocky outcroppings? or perhaps fields ablaze with the incredible colors of spring flowers? Do you realize that even a king's palace—incomparably lavish with magnificent trappings of silver and gold, ivory and pearls, and exquisite art and beauty in each detail—pales in comparison to the splendor of the dwelling place of the King of kings?

FROM **THE BOOK**

The wall was made of jasper, and the city was pure gold, as clear as glass. The wall of the city was built on foundation stones inlaid with twelve gems: the first was jasper, the second sapphire, the third agate, the fourth emerald, the fifth onyx, the sixth carnelian, the seventh chrysolite, the eighth beryl, the ninth topaz, the tenth chrysoprase, the eleventh jacinth, the twelfth amethyst.

The twelve gates were made of pearls—each gate from a single pearl! And the main street was pure gold, as clear as glass. *Revelation 21:18-21,* page 1263

Look, the home of God is now among his people! He will live with them, and they will be his people. God himself will be with them. He will remove all of their sorrows, and there will be no more death or sorrow or crying or pain. For the old world and its evils are gone forever. *Revelation 21:3-4,* page 1263

God so loved the world that he gave his only Son, so that everyone who believes in him will not perish but have eternal life. *John 3:16,* page 1047

This is the way to have eternal life—to know you, the only true God, and Jesus Christ, the one you sent to earth. *John 17:3,* page 1068

GOD'S PROMISE

There are many rooms in my Father's home, and I am going to prepare a place for you. If this were not so, I would tell you plainly. When everything is ready, I will come and get you, so that you will always be with me where I am. *John 14:2-3,* page 1065

ACTION POINT

Eternal life can be yours today. Once you choose to receive Christ's forgiveness and follow him, you can be certain that your destiny is heaven. What God has provided no one can take away. Let that thought bring you peace as you face today's trials.

Day 12

MARRIAGE

Marriage is a subject surrounded by conflicting messages in today's society. We hear alarming news about soaring divorce rates, while at the same time Bride *magazine is over 1,200 pages long. Recent scientific studies have been touting the benefits to health that good marriages provide, confirming the wisdom of* The Book, *which has been saying as much for two thousand years.*

FROM **THE BOOK**

As the Scriptures say, "A man leaves his father and mother and is joined to his wife, and the two are united into one." . . . So again I say, each man must love his wife as he loves himself, and the wife must respect her husband. *Ephesians 5:31, 33, page 1177*

Give honor to marriage, and remain faithful to one another in marriage. God will surely judge people who are immoral and those who commit adultery. *Hebrews 13:4,* page 1221

You husbands must give honor to your wives. Treat her with understanding as you live together. She may be weaker than you are, but she is your equal partner in God's gift of new life. If you don't treat her as you should, your prayers will not be heard. *1 Peter 3:7,* page 1230

You husbands must love your wives with the same love Christ showed the church. . . . In the same way, husbands ought to love their wives as they love their own bodies. For a man is actually loving himself when he loves his wife. *Ephesians 5:25, 28,* page 1177

I am my lover's, the one he desires. Come, my love, let us go out into the fields and spend the night among the wildflowers. Let us get us early and go out to the vineyards. Let us see whether the vines have budded, whether the blossoms have opened, and whether the pomegranates are in flower. And there I will give you my love. *Song of Songs 7:10-12,* page 679

GOD'S PROMISE

The man who finds a wife finds a treasure
and receives favor from the LORD.
Proverbs 18:22, page 653

ACTION POINT

Good marriages are important for a society's health, and the God of *The Book*
desires good marriages. If you are mar-
ried, dedicate your energy to bringing
respect, honor, and romance to your
union. Plan a date night, give a surprise
gift, and remember to state your apprecia-
tion of something in your spouse daily.

Day **13**

CHILDREN/FAMILY

With so many families being labeled dysfunctional, you may be wondering, What's the point? But a healthy family is a marvelous thing, providing a child with love, safety, and encouragement and building a foundation for a successful life. The Book has a lot to say about how to build a great family.

FROM **THE BOOK**

Children are a gift from the LORD; they are a reward from him. *Psalm 127:3,* page 630

Fathers, don't aggravate your children. If you do, they will become discouraged and quit trying. *Colossians 3:21,* page 1186

And now a word to you fathers. Don't make your children angry by the way you treat them. Rather, bring them up with the discipline and instruction approved by the Lord. *Ephesians 6:4,* page 1177

Honor your father and mother. Then you will live a long, full life in the land the LORD your God will give you. *Exodus 20:12,* page 82

Again I say, each man must love his wife as he loves himself, and the wife must respect her husband. *Ephesians 5:33,* page 1177

GOD'S PROMISE

Teach your children to choose the right path, and when they are older, they will remain upon it. *Proverbs 22:6,* page 656

ACTION POINT

Bless the children. Mother, father, grandmother, grandfather, aunt, uncle, stepparent, foster parent, guardian—whatever you are—give love and hope to a child today, "for the Kingdom of Heaven belongs to such as these" (Matthew 19:14).

FEAR AND COURAGE

For millions of people, fear is a formidable foe. Whether it stems from a real danger or is simply a crippling emotional bondage, fear can destroy peace and hold captive those tortured by it. How can we gain the courage to overcome our fears? By realizing that God is for his people and that he will never leave his children!

FROM **THE BOOK**

He will shield you with his wings. He will shelter you with his feathers. His faithful promises are your armor and protection. Do not be afraid of the terrors of the night, nor fear the dangers of the day, nor dread the plague that stalks in darkness, nor the disaster that strikes at midday. Though a thousand fall at your side, though ten thousand are dying around you, these evils will not touch you. But you will see it with your eyes; you will see how the wicked are punished.

    If you make the LORD your refuge, if

you make the Most High your shelter, no evil will conquer you; no plague will come near your dwelling. For he orders his angels to protect you wherever you go. They will hold you with their hands to keep you from striking your foot on a stone. . . .

The LORD says, "I will rescue those who love me. I will protect those who trust in my name. When they call on me, I will answer; I will be with them in trouble. I will rescue them and honor them. I will satisfy them with a long life and give them my salvation." *Psalm 91:4-12, 14-16,* page 613

Don't be afraid, for I am with you. Do not be dismayed, for I am your God. I will strengthen you. I will help you. I will uphold you with my victorious right hand. *Isaiah 41:10,* page 714

God has not given us a spirit of fear and timidity, but of power, love, and self-discipline. *2 Timothy 1:7,* page 1199

GOD'S PROMISE

Be strong and very courageous. Obey all the laws Moses gave you. Do not turn away from them, and you will be successful in everything you do. Study this Book of the Law continually. Meditate on it day and night so you may be sure to obey all that is written in it. Only then will you succeed. I command you—be strong and courageous! Do not be afraid or discouraged. For the LORD your God is with you wherever you go. *Joshua 1:7-9, page 231*

ACTION POINT

Write down these verses about fear and courage on some index cards. Hang one on a bathroom mirror; keep one in the car; place one on your desk and another in your wallet. Read the verses again and again. God will strengthen you through his Word, and you can be victorious as you face your fears.

Day **15**

HEALTH AND HEALING

Caring for our health—there's always something about it in the news. Diet. Exercise. E-coli. Medicare. AIDS. Technology has given us some marvelous advantages over previous generations, but we're also relearning some ancient wisdom about our health—including that our choices matter. What we plant is what we will harvest, and God desires that we harvest good health.

FROM **THE BOOK**

Because of your anger, my whole body is sick; my health is broken because of my sins. *Psalm 38:3,* page 586

Don't be impressed with your own wisdom. Instead, fear the LORD and turn your back on evil. Then you will gain renewed health and vitality. *Proverbs 3:7-8,* page 641

O LORD my God, I cried out to you for help, and you restored my health. *Psalm 30:2,* page 581

A vast crowd brought him the lame, blind, crippled, mute, and many others with physical difficulties, and they laid them before Jesus. And he healed them all. *Matthew 15:30, page 950*

GOD'S PROMISE

Praise the LORD, I tell myself, and never forget the good things he does for me. He forgives all my sins and heals all my diseases. *Psalm 103:2-3, page 617*

ACTION POINT

Healthy choices are smart choices. Holy living is healthy living. Ask God for power to follow through on healthy changes, and expect healing to follow from him.

ANGER

Road rage. Domestic violence. Hurtful words. Emotional outbursts. All of these remind us that many people carry around an enormous amount of anger. When we feel we have been wronged, how can we deal with the resulting anger in a way that does not harm others? The answer is found in The Book.

FROM **THE BOOK**

Don't copy the behavior and customs of this world, but let God transform you into a new person by changing the way you think. . . .

Don't just pretend that you love others. Really love them. Hate what is wrong. Stand on the side of the good. Love each other with genuine affection, and take delight in honoring each other. . . .

Be glad for all God is planning for you. Be patient in trouble, and always be prayerful. When God's children are in need, be the one to help them out. . . .

If people persecute you because you are a Christian, don't curse them; pray that God will bless them. When others are happy, be happy with them. If they are sad, share their sorrow. Live in harmony with each other. Don't try to act important, but enjoy the company of ordinary people. And don't think you know it all!

Never pay back evil for evil to anyone. Do things in such a way that everyone can see you are honorable. Do your part to live in peace with everyone, as much as possible. *Romans 12:2, 9-18,* page 1130

My dear brothers and sisters, be quick to listen, slow to speak, and slow to get angry. Your anger can never make things right in God's sight. *James 1:19-20,* page 1223

A gentle answer turns away wrath, but harsh words stir up anger. *Proverbs 15:1,* page 650

People with good sense restrain their anger; they earn esteem by overlooking wrongs. *Proverbs 19:11,* page 654

GOD'S PROMISE

Dear friends, never avenge yourselves. Leave that to God. For it is written, "I will take vengeance; I will repay those who deserve it," says the Lord. Instead, do what the Scriptures say: "If your enemies are hungry, feed them. If they are thirsty, give them something to drink, and they will be ashamed of what they have done to you." Don't let evil get the best of you, but conquer evil by doing good. *Romans 12:19-21,* page 1131

ACTION POINT

Conquer evil with good today. When you are wronged, take a moment to pray and to ask God to work forgiveness in your heart. Look for an opportunity to pay back an insult with a kind word or a traffic problem with a wave. Start a ripple of peace, and watch the effects in your life and in the lives of others.

PEACE

Peace. One of its meanings is "inner contentment; calm; serenity." In the late twentieth century, this is what so many long for: a calm place, a refuge, a sanctuary for the soul—you know, the ability to keep your head when others around you are losing theirs. Is there an oasis of the spirit that refreshes us even in the hurly-burly world we live in? The Book *shows us there is.*

FROM **THE BOOK**

You will keep in perfect peace all who trust in you, whose thoughts are fixed on you. *Isaiah 26:3,* page 699

The eternal God is your refuge, and his everlasting arms are under you. He thrusts out the enemy before you; it is he who cries, "Destroy them!" *Deuteronomy 33:27,* page 229

You are my rock and my fortress. For the honor of your name, lead me out of this peril. *Psalm 31:3,* page 581

My help comes from the LORD, who made the heavens and the earth! He will not let you stumble and fall; the one who watches over you will not sleep. *Psalm 121:2-3, page 629*

Those who live in the shelter of the Most High will find rest in the shadow of the Almighty. *Psalm 91:1, page 613*

Jesus said, "Come to me, all of you who are weary and carry heavy burdens, and I will give you rest." *Matthew 11:28, page 943*

GOD'S PROMISE

I am leaving you with a gift—peace of mind and heart. And the peace I give isn't like the peace the world gives. So don't be troubled or afraid. *John 14:27, page 1066*

ACTION POINT

Identify your "disturbers of the peace." Talk to God about your inability to handle them well. Ask him to send his peace into those situations.

Day 18

FINANCES

The funeral was noteworthy, for the deceased had been terribly wealthy. In the back of the room, two acquaintances spoke of the settlement of the will. "How much did he leave?" one asked. "All of it," said the other.

That story seems to characterize The Book's *approach to finances. While useful, money can't become a priority. It doesn't even enter eternity with us. Jesus said, "A person is a fool to store up earthly wealth but not have a rich relationship with God"* (Luke 12:21).

FROM **THE BOOK**

We didn't bring anything with us when we came into the world, and we certainly cannot carry anything with us when we die. So if we have enough food and clothing, let us be content. *1 Timothy 6:7-8, page 1198*

Remember the words of the Lord Jesus: "It is more blessed to give than to receive." *Acts 20:35, page 1105*

Tell those who are rich in this world not to be proud and not to trust in their money, which will soon be gone. But their trust should be in the living God, who richly gives us all we need for our enjoyment. Tell them to use their money to do good. They should be rich in good works and should give generously to those in need, always being ready to share with others whatever God has given them. *1 Timothy 6:17-18, page 1198*

GOD'S PROMISE

By doing this they will be storing up their treasure as a good foundation for the future so that they may take hold of real life. *1 Timothy 6:19, page 1198*

ACTION POINT

Invest in people. Souls are eternal. Count your blessings, and share with someone less fortunate. Be a blessing to someone today.

Day **19**

THE ENVIRONMENT

*We hear a lot these days about such things
as global warming, nuclear winter, and
polluted air and water. What is our role
in all of this? Can the environment be
protected and used at the same time? What
are the guidelines for wise management?
How will it all turn out? The Book gives us
God's perspective regarding creation and
our role in it.*

FROM **THE BOOK**

The earth is the LORD's, and everything in
it. The world and all its people belong to
him. *Psalm 24:1,* page 578

God blessed them and told them, "Multi-
ply and fill the earth and subdue it. Be
masters over the fish and birds and all the
animals." *Genesis 1:28,* page 4

To Adam he said, "Because you listened
to your wife and ate the fruit I told you
not to eat, I have placed a curse on the
ground. All your life you will struggle to

scratch a living from it. It will grow thorns and thistles for you, though you will eat of its grains. All your life you will sweat to produce food." *Genesis 3:17-19, page 6*

Against its will, everything on earth was subjected to God's curse. All creation anticipates the day when it will join God's children in glorious freedom from death and decay. *Romans 8:20-21, page 1125*

And God has also commanded that the heavens and the earth will be consumed by fire on the day of judgment. . . .
    You should look forward to that day and hurry it along—the day when God will set the heavens on fire and the elements will melt away in the flames. *2 Peter 3:7, 12, page 1235*

GOD'S PROMISE

We are looking forward to the new heavens and new earth he has promised, a world where everyone is right with God. *2 Peter 3:13, page 1235*

ACTION POINT

The Book proclaims that a renewed earth will emerge from the fires of God's judgment. In the meantime we are given the responsibility to carefully manage the resources at hand. Be good to the earth, not because it's our mother, but because it's the home we are to care for. Act wisely, but remember, God is in control of his creation.

COMFORT/HOPE

*"Where there's life, there's hope." So goes the
old saying. One can never predict how we
will respond in a crisis, and there's no cer-
tainty how God may step in to change the
course of events. So, given these two facts,
we plow on in hope, defeating despair with
our faith.*

FROM **THE BOOK**

The LORD is my shepherd; I have everything I need. . . .

Even when I walk through the dark val-
ley of death, I will not be afraid, for you
are close beside me. Your rod and your
staff protect and comfort me. *Psalm 23:1,
4, page 578*

I prayed to the LORD, and he answered
me, freeing me from all my fears. . . .

The LORD hears his people when they
call to him for help. He rescues them from
all their troubles. The LORD is close to the

brokenhearted; he rescues those who are crushed in spirit. *Psalm 34:4, 17-18,* page 583

When doubts filled my mind, your comfort gave me renewed hope and cheer. *Psalm 94:19,* page 614

Give all your worries and cares to God, for he cares about what happens to you. *1 Peter 5:7,* page 1232

GOD'S PROMISE

When you go through deep waters and great trouble, I will be with you. When you go through rivers of difficulty, you will not drown! When you walk through the fire of oppression, you will not be burned up; the flames will not consume you. *Isaiah 43:2,* page 716

ACTION POINT

The Lord is the triumphant God of seemingly lost causes and hopeless situations. Take a few minutes to list your worries, doubts, fears, and troubles. Ask God to comfort you in each of these areas.

THE FUTURE/
THE END OF TIME

If you had a dollar for every wrong prediction about the end of the world and laid them end to end—well, let's just say you'd have a lot of dollars. A yearning to know the future spawns psychic hotlines and futurist seminars in the hope that we can control our destiny. Yet it takes but one natural disaster to remind us we are often at the mercy of unforeseen events. One accident can change forever the course we have set for ourselves. The future arrives daily, ready or not.

FROM **THE BOOK**

You may wonder, "How will we know whether the prophecy is from the LORD or not?" If the prophet predicts something in the LORD's name and it does not happen, the LORD did not give the message. That prophet has spoken on his own and need not be feared. *Deuteronomy 18:21-22,* page 210

Do not forget the things I have done throughout history. For I am God— I alone! I am God, and there is no one else like me. Only I can tell you what is going to happen even before it happens. Everything I plan will come to pass, for I do whatever I wish. *Isaiah 46:9-10, page 720*

But the day of the Lord will come as unexpectedly as a thief. Then the heavens will pass away with a terrible noise, and everything in them will disappear in fire, and the earth and everything on it will be exposed to judgment. *2 Peter 3:10, page 1235*

GOD'S PROMISE

The King will say to those on the right, "Come, you who are blessed by my Father, inherit the Kingdom prepared for you from the foundation of the world." *Matthew 25:34, page 964*

ACTION POINT

If you want to know the future, check with the Author. He's written the road map in the pages of *The Book*. One thing we know for certain about the future—we'll spend it somewhere.

FOR MORE INFORMATION

Congratulations! You have begun a wonderful habit; now keep the momentum going!

God's promises are true and powerful, and they will improve life for you and your family. Reading *The Book* each day puts God's promises in your heart and mind. *The Book* tells us that our faith is built by hearing and learning the Word of God. So keep at it! This is the best habit you will ever acquire.

Let us know how you have enjoyed *The Book: 21 Day Habit.* Perhaps a situation in your life was resolved as a result of your readings. Or maybe you discovered peace with God for the very first time in your life. We would love to hear from you.

For more readings and further information, visit us at *The Book* Web site:

ireadTheBook.com

Or write to us at:

The Book Project, SHB - 415
977 Centerville Turnpike
Virginia Beach, Virginia 23463-0001

FROM INFORMATION TO UNDERSTANDING.

PRESENTS

Watch daily at 10 a.m. and 11 p.m. on
the FOX Family Channel or check local listings.

In need of prayer? Call your local church or
the National Counseling Center at 1-800-759-0700.
24 Hours A Day, 7 Days A Week.

Visit www.cbn.org, one of America's top Christian resource sites.